Animal Peculiarity Part 5

By T.P Just

~~~

Copyright © 2010 by Terence Just. All rights reserved.

I0436335

Get All The Books In The Series:

Animal Peculiarity Part 1
Animal Peculiarity Part 2
Animal Peculiarity Part 3
Animal Peculiarity Part 4
Animal Peculiarity Part 5
Animal Peculiarity Part 6
Animal Peculiarity Part 7
Animal Peculiarity Part 8
Just Enterprises

Table of Contents

1 Introduction

The unique characteristics of animals is a miscellany of facts, genuine or supposed, gleamed from earlier and contemporary Greek writers (No Latin writer is once named) and to a limited extent from his own observation to illustrate the habits of the animal world.

We are of course prepared to encounter much that modern science rejects, but the general tone with its search after the picturesque, the startling, even the miraculous, would justify us in ranking Aelian with the paradoxical, rather than with the sober exponents of natural history.

Mythology, mariners' yarns, vulgar superstitions, the ascertained facts of nature—all serve to adorn a tale and, on occasion, to point a moral. His religion is the popular stoicism of the age. Aleian repeatedly affirms his belief in the gods and in divine providence; the wisdom and beneficence of Nature are held up to veneration; the folly and selfishness of man are contrasted with the untaught virtues of the animal world. Some animals, to be sure, have their failings, but he chooses rather to dwell upon their good qualities, devotion, courage, self-sacrifice, gratitude. Again, animals are guided by reason, and from them we may learn contentment, control of the passions, and calm in the face of death.

His primary object is to entertain and while so doing to convey instruction in the most agreeable form. Some might find fault with his random and piece-meal handling of his theme-of which he is well aware, and he defends himself with the plea that a frequent change of topic helps to maintain the reader's interest and saves him from boredom.

As to the permanent value of his work he has no misgivings and since we have been informed that his writings were much admired, we may assume that they appealed to cultivated circles in a way that the voluminous and possibly arid compilations of grammarians did not.

Now I am well aware of the labour that others have expended on this subject, yet I have collected all the materials that I could; I have clothed them in untechnical language, and am persuaded that my achievement is a treasure far from negligible. So if anyone considers them profitable, let him make use of them; anyone who does not consider them so may give them to his father to keep and attend to.

2 The Hare

The Hare has certain innate- characteristics. For one thing it sleeps with its eyelids open; for another it proclaims its age when it half shows certain apertures.
Also it carries some of its young half-formed in its womb, some it is in process of bearing, others it has already borne.

3 Fishes and their leaders

All the large fishes, with the exception of the Shark, require a leader, and are guided by its eyes. The leader is a small, slim fish with an elongated head, but its tail is narrow, according to the authorities on the subject.

But whether Nature has conferred upon each large fish the aforesaid guide, or whether it associates with the large fish of its own free will out of friendliness, I am unable to say, but I prefer to believe that this is done under the compulsion of Nature, for this fish never swims by itself, but moves in front of the large fish's head and is its leader and, as it were, tiller. For instance, it foresees and takes previous notice of everything on behalf of the large fish; it forewarns it of everything by the tip of its tail, and by its contact signals to the fish, keeping it away from what is to be feared but leading it on to what will feed it.

And by some invisible sign it warns the fish that its pursuers have designs upon it, and gives timely indication of those spots which a creature of its size ought not to approach, if it is not to be surrounded and perish utterly on some reef.

So then the first essential for the life of the largest of creatures is the smallest. And it seems that when the large fish becomes very fat it can no longer see nor hear, the vast bulk of its flesh being an obstacle to sight and to hearing.

But the 'leader' is never seen apart from the large fish; if however, with its responsibility for the services described above, it dies first, then the large fish is bound to die also.

4 The Chameleon

The Chameleon is not disposed to remain of was one and the
same colour for men to see and recognize, but it conceals itself
by misleading and deceiving the eye of the beholder.
Thus, if you come across one that appears black, it changes its
semblance to green, as though it had changed its clothes; then
again it assumes a bluish-grey tint and appears different, like
an actor who puts on another mask or another garment.
This being so, one might say that even nature, though she
does not boil anyone down nor apply drugs, like a Medea or a
Circe, is also a sorceress.

5 The Pilot-fish

You must know that the Pilot-fish frequents the open sea and loves to dwell in the depths more than all others of which we have heard tell. But either it detests the land or the land detests the fish.

Well, when vessels are cleaving the mid-ocean these Pilot- fish swim up as though they were in love with them and attend them like a bodyguard, circling this way and that as they gambol and leap.

Now the passengers are of course totally unable to tell how far they are from land, and even the sailors themselves are frequently mistaken as to the true fact.

The Pilot-fish however can tell from a long- way off, like a keen-scented hound which immediately gets wind of the prey, and then they are no longer so captivated by the vessel as to stay at her side, but has acquired its name, for those who have had experience call it the Ship-holder.

In Homer skill in treating the wounded and persons in need of medicine goes back as far as the third generation of pupil and master. Thus Patrols', son of Menoetius, is taught the healing art by Achilles and Achilles, son of Peleus, is taught by Cheiron, son of Cronus.

And heroes and children of the gods learnt about the nature of roots, the use of different herbs, the concocting of drugs, spells to reduce inflammations, the way to staunch blood, and everything else that they knew. And moreover there are discoveries which men of a later age have made.

The Elephant

But that Nature really has no need of these ingenuities is proved by the case of the Elephant; for instance, when it is assailed with spears and a shower of arrows, it eats the flower of the olive or the actual oil, and then shakes off every missile that has pierced it and is sound and whole again.

6 The Bear and its Cub

The Bear is unable to produce a cub, nor would anyone allow, on seeing its offspring immediately after birth, that it had borne a living thing.

Yet the Bear has been in labour, though the lump of nondescript flesh has no distinguishing mark, no form, and no shape.

But the mother loves it and recognises it as her child, keeps it warm beneath her thighs, smooths it with her tongue, fashions it into limbs, and little by little brings it into shape; and when you see it you would say that this is a Bear's cub.

The Oxen of Erythrae

All Bulls have inflexible and rigid horns, and this is why, just as a man puts passion into his weapons, so a bull puts passion into its horns. But the oxen of Erythrae can move their horns as they do their ears.

7 The Snakes of Ethiopia and Phrygia

The land of Ethiopia (the place Where the gods bathe, celebrated by Homer under the name of Ocean, is an excellent and desirable neighbor), this land, I say, is the mother of the very largest Serpents.

For, you must know, they attain to a length of one hundred and eighty feet, and they are not called by the name of any species, but people say that they kill elephants and these serpents rival the longest-lived animals.

Thus far the accounts from Ethiopia, But according to accounts from Phrygia there are Serpents in Phrygia too, and these grow to a length of sixty feet, and every day in mid-summer some time after noon they creep out of their lairs. And on the banks of the river Rhyndacus while supporting part of their coils on the ground, they raise all the rest of their body and, steadily and silently extending their neck open their mouth and attract birds by their breath, as it were by a spell.

And the birds descend feathers and all, into their stomach, drawn in by the Serpents breathing. And these singular practices they continue until sun-down; next, the Serpents hide and lie in wait for the flocks, and as they return to the sheepfolds from the pasture they fall upon them, and after a terrible slaughter they have frequently killed the herdsmen as well, thus obtaining a generous and abundant feast.

8 The Sprat

Sprats are born of mud; they neither beget nor are begotten of one another, but when the mud in the sea becomes altogether slimy and thick and turns black, it is warmed by some inexplicable and life-giving principle, undergoes a transformation, and is changed into innumerable living creatures.

The Sprats are these creatures, resembling Worms which are generated in mire and filth. And as soon as born, Sprats are excellent swimmers, and they do it naturally. Then by some mysterious agency they are led to safe places where they will find shelter and protection, so that it will be possible for them to live.

And their place of refuge is likely to be either some rock that rises to a great height or what are called 'baker's pots'; these would be rocks full of embrasures which the waves have in time eaten away until they have become hollow.

These then are the retreats to which Nature has pointed them so that they shall not be battered and demolished by the swell of the sea; for they have little strength and are powerless to resist the impact of the Waves. They need no food; indeed it is enough for them to lick one another.

The way to catch them is to use exceedingly fine thread with thin pieces from the warp of garments laced in. this device should be quite sufficient for catching and securing them, though for the capture of other fish it would be utterly inadequate.

9 The Lizard, its vitality

Should you strike a Lizard with a stick and either on purpose or by accident cut it in two, neither of the two parts is killed, but each moves separately and by itself, and lives, both the one and the other trailing on two feet.

Then when the parts meet-for the forepart frequently unites with the hinder- the two join up and coalesce after their separation. And the Lizard, now one body, although a scar gives evidence of What it has suffered, yet runs about and maintains its former method of life exactly like one of its kind that has had no such experience.

The Asp, its poison

The poison of serpents is a thing to be dreaded, but that of the Asp is far worse. Nor are remedies and antidotes easy to discover, however ingenious one may be at beguiling and dispelling acute pains. Yet after all there is in man also a certain mysterious poison, and this is how it has been discovered.

Human spittle

If you capture a Viper and grasp its neck very firmly and with a strong hand, and then open its mouth and spit into it, the spittle slides down into its belly and has so disastrous an effect upon it as to cause the Viper to rot away. From this you see how foul can be the bite of one man to another and as dangerous as the bite of any beast.

10 The Ant

In the summertime when the harvest is in and the corn is being threshed on the threshing-floor, Ants assemble in companies, going in single file or two abreast-indeed they sometimes go three abreast-after quitting their homes and customary shelters.

Then they pick out some of the barley and the wheat and all follow the same track. And some go to collect the grain, others carry the load, and they get out of each other's way with the utmost deference and consideration, especially those that are not laden for the benefit of those that are.

Then they return to their dwellings and fill the pits in their store-chamber after boring through the middle of each grain. What falls out becomes the Ant's meal at the time; what is left is infertile.

This is a device on the part of these excellent and thrifty housekeepers to prevent the intact grain from putting out shoots and sprouting afresh when the rains have surrounded them, and to preserve themselves in that case from falling victims during the winter to want of food and to famine, and their zeal from being blunted. It is to Nature then that Ants too owe these and other fortunate gifts.

11 The Eagle

At no time does the Eagle need water or long for a dusting-place; he is on the contrary superior to thirst and looks for no medicine for weariness from any outside source, but scorning water and repose he cleaves the atmosphere and gazes with piercing eye from the vast expanse of heaven on high.

And at the mere sound of those rushing wings even that most intrepid of all creatures, the great serpent, dives at once into its den and is glad to disappear. And this is the way in which the Eagle tests the legitimacy of his young ones.

He plants them, while they are still tender and unfledged, facing the rays of the sun, and if one of them blinks, unable to endure the brightness of the rays, it is thrust out of the nest and banished from that hearth.

If however it can face the sun quite unmoved, it is above suspicion and is enrolled among the legitimate offspring, since the celestial fire is an impartial and uncorrupt register of its origin.

12 The Ostrich

The Ostrich is covered with thick feathers, but its nature does not permit it to rise from the ground and mount aloft into the sky. Yet its speed is very great, and when it spreads its Wings on either side, the Wind meeting them causes them to belly like sails.

The Bustard

Among birds the Bustard is, I am told, the most fond of horses. And the proof of this is that it scorns all other animals that live in field or glen, but that when it catches sight of a horse, it delights to fly up to it and to keep it company, just like men who are devoted to horses.

The Fly

When a Fly falls into the water, though it is of all creatures the most daring, yet it can neither run upon the surface nor swim, and hence it drowns. If however you pick out the dead body, sprinkle ashes upon it, and place it in the sunshine, you will bring the Fly to life again.

13 The Cockerel

If you want to add a Cockerel, whether bought or presented, to your flock of domestic fowls, you must not release him nor let him loose at random and in a casual way; otherwise he will immediately desert and go back to his own kin and mates, however far away from them he be. So you must set upon him a guard and fetters more invisible than those of Hephaestus in Homer.

What I prescribe is this. Place the table at which you eat, in the open, seize the Cockerel, and when you have taken him three times round the aforesaid platform, then let him go free to wander with the fowls of the house. He will not go away any more than if he were chained up.

14 The Salamander

The Salamander is not indeed one of those fire-born creatures
like the so-called 'Fire-flies,' yet it is as bold as they and
encounters the flame and is eager to fight it like an enemy.
And the proof of this is as follows.

Its haunts are among artisans and craftsmen who work at the
forge. Now so long as their fire is at full blast and they have it
to help their craft and to share their skill, they pay, not the
smallest attention to this animal.

When however the fire goes out or languishes and the bellows
blow in vain, then at once they know full well that the
aforesaid creature is working against them.

Accordingly they track it down and exact vengeance; and then
the fire is lit, is easily coaxed up, and does not go out,
provided it is kept fed with the usual material.

15 The Swan and its song

The Swan is assigned by poets and many prose writers as
servant to Apollo, but in what other relation it stands to music
and song I do not know. Yet the ancients believed that when it
has sung 'what is called its 'swan-song,' it dies.

In that case Nature honours it more highly than it does noble
and upright men, and rightly so, for while others praise and
lament them, Swans praise or, if you will, lament themselves.

16 The Crocodile

Many writers tell us about the size of the Crocodile both -
when fully grown and when first hatched, and further, about
its tongue, and whether it moves its jaw and which jaw it
closes upon the other.

There are those too who have observed that this animal lays as
many eggs as the days during which it sits upon them before
hatching out its young.

And I have myself heard that when a Crocodile dies a
scorpion is born from it; and they do say that it has a sting in
its tail which is full of poison.

17 The Cinnamon bird

If these facts are certain and beyond dispute, then let this story from India carry conviction. What I propose to tell has been brought from thence by report and is as follows.
I have learnt from the son of Nicomachus that there is a bird named Cinnamon like the plant, and that the bird brings this plant, which is named after it, to the Indians, but that these people have no knowledge Where and how the plant grows.

18 The Ibis and Clysters

The Egyptians assert that knowledge of clysters and intestinal purges is derived from no discovery of man's, but they commonly affirm that it was the Ibis that taught them this remedy. And how it instructed those who were the first to see it, some other shall tell.

And I have also heard that it knows when the moon is waxing and when waning; and I cannot deny that I have learnt from some source that it diminishes or increases its food according as the goddess herself diminishes or increases.

The Sting-ray

The Sting-ray in the sea has a far fiercer and more dangerous sting than all other creatures. The proof is that if you fix it in a flourishing tree that has grown to a great height, then without any delay, before any time has elapsed, the tree immediately withers. And if you allow the sting to scratch any living creature, you kill it at once.

19 The Shrew-mouse

So long as the Shrew-mouse proceeds as chance directs, it can live, and Nature is on friendly terms with it, unless it is overtaken by misfortune from some other quarter and is killed.

When however it falls into a rut, it is caught, so to say, in quite invisible fetters and dies. The remedy for a man who has been bitten by a Shrew-mouse is as follows.

Take some sand from the Wheel-track, sprinkle it on the bite, and it cures him immediately.

Get All The Books In The Series:

www.ingramcontent.com/pod-product-compliance
Lightning Source LLC
Chambersburg PA
CBHW050919290526
45792CB00002B/814